THIS WORKS

DR. ROBERT A. RUSSELL

Audio Enlightenment Press

Giving Voice to the Wisdom of the Ages

Printed in the United States of America

First Printing, 2022
ISBN 978-1-941489-91-8

www.RobertARussell.Org

Table of Contents

To my friend, James J. Divine, this little book is affectionately dedicated. He leaves behind him the beautiful benediction of a life that was mysteriously complete. His conscientious loyalty to what he believed to be right and true, his sincerity and purity of purpose will be a constant source of inspiration to all those who knew him.

May Perpetual light shine upon him.

This Works

"My Father worketh hitherto and I work."

SEVEN MILLION DOLLARS IN ANSWER TO PRAYER

"George Müller took two or three promises in the Bible where God gives assurance of His care for orphans and for those who cry out to Him in need and multiplying these, he stepped into the realization that God meant what He said. Then with that realization he asked God for help for his orphans, and over seven million dollars came to him. He said, "When I asked the Father for five hundred dollars, it came; when I asked for five thousand dollars—it came; I am convinced that if I should ever ask for five million dollars it would come just as easily."

When asked what was the secret of his phenomenal success in prayer, George Müller replied, "There was a day when I utterly died—UTTERLY DIED—died to George Müller, his opinions, tastes, will; died to the world, its approval and censure; died to the blame or approval of brothers and friends—and since then I have studied only to show myself approved of God."

We tell this story (well known to most of the Christian world) at 'the beginning of our study because it contains the key to all that follows—the keynote of the teachings of Jesus. The secret of George Müller's success in Spiritual work is the secret of any other man or woman who has successfully solved his or her every day problems through the application of Spiritual Law. **If one will put God back at the center of living by dying to himself or letting the human mind die, there is**

1

nothing, absolutely nothing that he cannot have, cannot be or cannot do.

When one trusts God completely with everything in his life and takes no thought for his life, body, or what he puts on the body, no thought for what he eats or drinks, and no thought for tomorrow or the future, he is letting the human mind die.

The vital need in religion today is a deeper consciousness of God's Presence and a more intelligent understanding of Spiritual Law. As man is both divine and human, both spiritual and physical, both mental and material, he can succeed in his endeavors only when the two operate jointly, or together. The teachings of Jesus are both reasonable, practical and provable. They can be applied successfully to everyday problems only when they are consciously employed.

It should be noted however, that our efforts toward Spiritual re-adjustment will have no chance of success until our multiple selves have been united or synchronized with God. Since the three phases of our being complement and are an extension of every other phase, it is impossible for man to live successfully in any one part of his being at the expense of any other part.

Successful living and achievement depend absolutely upon the unity and perfect coordination and cooperation of all three.

Satisfactory material conditions and the ability to solve problems can be built up only as man, Christ and God work hand in hand, only as they operate jointly. The great secret of opulence, health and power is to keep the mind one-pointed toward God and out of conflict with the world. "A controlled mind is a successful mind."

We may share today Christ's victory over the world only as we have learned to share His victory over Himself. "It can come only as we accept the **'Kingdom of God'** teaching as a way of life — as 'totalitarian' relative to the life of a Christian — as Naziism is totalitarian for Hitler's followers or as Fascism is totalitarian for the followers of Mussolini or as Russian communism is totalitarian for the Soviets. **'The Kingdom of God'** is Christian Totalitarianism, which simply means that it contains a rule of life for every part of man's being — a co-ordinating principle."

Totalitarianism means total identification with the principle which you represent, as when Jesus stood before Caiaphas, Pilate and the chief priests and again at His trial when it was revealed that Christ and the Kingdom of God had merged and were a single issue. This identity is made clear and was boldly declared in the face of every problem and adversary that confronted Him. It must be so with you. You will not stand before Caiaphas, Pilate and the chief priests. You will not have to carry a cross to Calvary because that has already been done for you. Your Chief Priests will be all of the problems in your life, and your cross will be the human mind which hides the Kingdom of God and keeps the needful things from you.

The supreme need of religion is not more books, preachers, teachers or practitioners but more consecration and dedication to the Kingdom of God on the part of those who call themselves students and followers of the Christ. If truth is to survive and prove Itself in human life it must match the heroic abandon and consecration of Totalitarianism. We must live to an end and give ourselves completely to it. To every temptation to compromise with evil we must be able to say with Jesus, "To this end was I born and for this cause came I into the world, **that I might bear witness unto the Truth.**"

The Kingdom of Heaven may be likened to a great irresistible and powerful magnet. The magnet is impersonal and unthinking. The Kingdom of Heaven would draw all men into it and keep them therein, if they would become as little children (let the human or adulterous mind die). "But as in magnetism, except a material possesses within itself certain properties, it will not respond to the magnetic influence. Yet the potency of the magnet remains unimpaired." "It is your Father's good pleasure to give you the Kingdom." Indeed He has given it already. The Kingdom of God contains all things within itself. It is within you, around you, above you and beneath you but you can take possession of it (personify it) only as you become conscious or aware that it is. Like attracts like. **You can live in the Kingdom of God and enjoy its benefits only as you build up and maintain a state of mind or consciousness which corresponds exactly to it.** After all "what can we see or acquire but what we are?"

Jesus likened the Kingdom of God to a "mustard seed." It is potential in every man. It is something that was planted in him in the beginning and grows up in him just to the extent that he recognizes, realizes and cultivates it. If he does not recognize it, cultivate and act upon it, it is like the seed that fell upon stony ground and could not grow. God's Power is **revealed,** not reflected nor transmitted. The Kingdom of God must be expressed. Before It can appear It must have a body. "Now are we the sons of God, and it doth not yet appear what we shall be, but we know that, when He shall appear we shall be like Him." When we give God our brains to think with, our eyes to see with, our ears to hear with, our mouths to speak with and our bodies to act with, then we shall know that the Kingdom of God is within us and that we are in it. We shall see Him as **He is.** We shall see ourselves as we are. We shall know that personality and God have no separate being—that they are one, "two manifestations of the same thing. **God is manifest**

and He is in His manifestation." He will be revealed just to the degree that man acknowledges the spirit of all things and thanks God for it. The spirit of a thing (the positive quality) is always good and to steadfastly behold the spirit of a thing is to call it forth or cause it to appear. To perceive the Truth, to grasp it, to hold it and use it, in the face of all negative appearances to the contrary, is Christian TOTALITARIANISM.

The Truth does not start with man, It is man's answer or response to God. The first line of the first book of the Bible says, "In the beginning GOD." And the first command that comes to us from God is · the command to put Him first. Because He is first, we are bidden to put Him first—first in our thought, first in our acts, first in our affection and first in our will. "Thou shalt put God first. Thou shalt not put anyone else or anything else above Him or alongside of Him. Thou shalt put all things under Him." **To acknowledge God, to know nothing but His Presence in every person, place and thing, is to acknowledge the highest and to call it forth.** The promise is, that "ye shall receive power after that the Holy Ghost is come upon you" (after the three phases of our being have been brought into complete cooperation with one another). "And ye shall be witnesses unto **Me."**

"I am God and besides me there is none else." I am All-in-All. I am All Presence. When we speak of Omnipresence we naturally think of God as being every where equally present—In all—through all—over all and under all. "Heaven and earth," says the Psalmist, "are full of Thee." There is nothing but God. There is nothing but His Presence and His Power.

Where do we look to find God? The answer is, anywhere and everywhere. God is wherever you look. God is every thing you behold. OMNIPRESENCE means that every thing and everybody you behold is God. Does that statement stretch your credulity? Does it sound inconsistent and far-fetched? Does it mean that if you look at a sick man whose body is racked with pain and disease that you are seeing God? It certainly does and if you did not have pain and disease in your own consciousness · you could not see them in another.

"Turn ye and look unto me, for I am God and beside me there is none else." The sick man is not sick because he is sick, the poor man is not poor because he is poor but because he does not behold God as He is, because he thinks of himself as something else. Does his sickness and poverty change God? Does it affect Him? Not at all. "God hath made man perfect," says the scriptures, and man is just as perfect when dying from some dread disease as when he was born. The only thing that ails him is that he does not "SEE HIM (GOD) AS HE IS." The only thing that is sick is his viewpoint. He is seeing something else and believing something else, and since he demonstrates his belief on all occasions he has the appearance of dying. In the human mind he does not have the spiritual properties within himself which causes God to appear as He is. What are these spiritual qualities which, if he had, would save him? **The total vision and understanding of God.**

Jesus touched on this same point when He said, "whom the world (human mind) cannot receive, because it seeth Him not, neither knoweth Him." You will understand how important true vision is and why Jesus said, "Judge not according to appearances," when you realize that eighty percent of the people in the world think with their eyes.

"My children," said an old man to his boys scared by a figure in a dark entry, "you will never see anything worse than yourselves."

"If thine eye be single," said the Master, "thy whole body shall be full of light;" and again, "let your light so shine before men that they may see your good works and glorify your Father who is in Heaven." Until the Light shines, God cannot appear. What we call demonstration is really nothing more than our ability to hold, as a specific image, the positive condition which a negative condition represents until that object has been reproduced in material form. "Let your light shine" means to keep your vision one-pointed and total toward God. **Your mind is the window through which you must see God. It must be kept clean and bright.**

"Look again," says the prophet and keep looking until you can see what is actually there. Can you see God in the devil that is making a hell of your life? Can you see Him in the problem which is driving you to distraction? Can you see Him in the blind eyes and the deaf ears, in the disease that is destroying your body? Do you see Him as **HE IS?** Do you see the positive quality which every negative quality suggests or are you judging according to the appearances of the human mind? Do you call the undesirable **God,** or do you call it something else? What are you trying to escape from? Is it problems and limitations or is it "low visibility?" Jesus did not say that you were to make the light shine but to LET IT SHINE.

"By their works, and not by their words, ye shall know them." It doesn't matter what you are seeing at the present time, from now on you must call it God. That is Christian TOTALITARIANISM. "If I make my bed in hell, thou art there." Keep reminding yourself that everything and everybody is God. Know that at the other end of every negative condition is the positive condition or God. The Creative Principle is there and only waiting for the reversal of your thought to bring the good into being. As you give your mind to the positive, you overcome the negative. Call everything God and focus your attention upon the positive which each negative suggests until you believe that it is God. You must do this in spite of all appearances to the contrary. The promise is that "He will keep him in perfect peace whose mind is stayed upon thee," — upon the positive. **Be positive.** Think positively. Speak positively. Act positively. "Look again" and "thine eyes shall behold the King in all His beauty."

"The eyes of the Christ were clear first of all to Truth. He did not permit their sight to be clouded by the slightest dwelling upon evil. "If thine eye be single (if you see only God), thy whole body shall be full of light. But if thine eye be evil (double), how great is the darkness!" The single eye is the total eye. It is the eye that sees only the good and the positive in every thing and magnifies that good by admitting no other evidence. "Every evil to which we do not succumb is a benefactor."

Jesus said, "No man, having put his hand to the plow and looking back is fit for the Kingdom of God." "He that is not with me is against me." If contrary evidence is admitted when one is seeking to demonstrate, the vision is distorted and the result will be defective. **The Truth that makes us free is the ability to stay the mind upon God and to see Him in every thing and everybody.** Circumstances, on the other hand, cannot change until we first have a state of mind that will produce them. When the imaged object produces in us a consciousness of itself, then it will be expressed outwardly in form.

Knowing that the highest price man ever pays for anything is to have it given to him, St. Paul said, "work out your own salvation." It is wise and timely advice for **it is an invariable**

law of the universe that man can have and retain only those things which are like or related to his own consciousness. When you are told to "work out your own salvation" it is as if you were told to eat your own food and drink your own water and breathe your own air. Just as no one else can think for you, breathe for you or eat for you, so no one else can save you or solve your personal problems. **Each man must contact God and employ the Higher faculties of the mind by and for himself.** Emerson says, "over all things that are agreeable to his nature and genius, the man has the highest right. Every where he may take what belongs to his spiritual estate, nor can he take any thing else though all doors were open, nor can all the force of men hinder him from taking so much."

Instead of seeking salvation in the jungle of metaphysical diagnosis and the babblings of un-illumined teachers who tell you that you can have the good things of life remaining as you are, it would be better to develop that state of mind which can give them to you – it would be better to deserve them. If you deserve the things you seek you will get them. If you do not deserve them all the teachers, priests, philosophers and metaphysicians in the world cannot give them to you. **What you deserve by right of consciousness you will have.** Conversely, what you do not deserve even God Himself cannot give you.

Christ is not a failure because you are content to know Him in the human mind. God is not a failure because you are sick, poor, unhappy or distressed. Shakespeare is not a failure because the majority are content with cheap novels and salacious stories. Edison is not a failure because people still use tallow candles and kerosene lamps. The failure is in ourselves that we have failed to employ methods of thinking and living which will produce new ideas and new conditions, and the means by which all our personal problems can be solved. We have yet to prove that the Kingdom of God is within us and that we can live in it now. "If the waters of a river are polluted, you cannot cleanse them by planting rose bushes on the river banks; you must go all the way back and clean the springs from which they flow." If your body is diseased, your hearing impaired or your vision dull, you cannot heal them by the repetition of beautiful words or statements of Truth. You must go beneath the surface to the soul and change its response. You must become totalitarian toward God.

If you really want to change conditions, heal your body and increase your income, then you must go clear back to the source of your difficulties which is a state of mind or consciousness. As the scriptures tell us we must stop . . . "walking in the vanity of our own mind, having the understanding darkened, being alienated from the life of God through the ignorance that is in us because of the blindness of our heart." Since all outward experiences are but the products of inner mental experiences, **we can only build desirable or satisfactory material conditions by first producing corresponding states of consciousness** — or "mental situations to be reproduced in the material." "Be ye transformed by the renewing of your mind." There is no other way.

Can you be cured? No! **You can only awake to the eternal and unchanging health which you already have.**

Can you be supplied with the good things of life which now seem to be lacking in your experience? No! **You can only awake to "all things" which you already have.** The only difference between "life more abundant" and life less abundant is a wrong perspective or negative state of mind. Both the positive and the negative are determined by the individual himself—by the subjective trend of his thought. "Our eyes are holden that we cannot see things that stare us in the face, until the hour arrives when the mind is ripened; then we behold them, and the time when we saw them not is like a dream."

What does it mean to "work out your own salvation?" It means to stop building disease and limitation, to give up all the enervating habits of living and thinking which are the causes of these conditions and to remove all the handicaps to the perfection and plenty which God is so constantly pouring forth into our lives. Yes, it means more. It means to transform all negative states of mind into positive ones—as when St. Paul said, to "overcome evil with good." When this is done, and not before then, nature will return to normal and man will enter again into perfect balance with God, man and the world. Until this is done however, our affirmations and study of Truth will do us little permanent good. Like medicine, they may give us a measure of temporary relief but health and supply cannot stay with us until rational thinking and living habits have been substituted for the irrational ones which caused all our difficulties. We repeat then, that when this is done and not before then, the good things of life, health, supply, peace and happiness will re-appear or return automatically.

Salvation comes to those who think with the mind of Christ. It comes to those who have learned to discriminate. **The riches of the Kingdom of Heaven are given only to those who think God's thoughts and obey His will.**

Emancipation is the reward of surrender and awareness. It comes to those who know and know that they know. Know what? Know that "God being perfect, made a perfect world, and planned that everything in it should be good, and all activity in it should be good. God is always carrying out that program, except where man thinks on some negative condition, and thereby forces the law to bring it to him, thus interfering with God's plan of bringing only good to him."

There is only one mental disease which is unawareness or ignorance and there is only one physical disease from which all other diseases spring. Its name is Enervation. Living in enervation is like riding on the rims. It is using nerve energy in excess of normal production. Its causes are legion but chiefly it is brought about by intemperance overeating, over-stimulation, mental friction, fear, worry, hurry, impatience, self-indulgence, dissatisfaction, anger, passion, pride, egotism, gossip, lying, jealousy, deception, self-pity, criticism, betrayal of confidences, abusing the credulity of friends, shock, selfishness, envy and grief. These are just a few of the causes of enervation which in time poison the blood stream and build so-called incurable disease in the body.

The wise Truth student will build from the bottom up. He will remove the negative mental hazards and correct the abnormal and perverted appetites first. "God hath made man perfect but man hath sought out many inventions." Please make a mental note of this and keep it foremost in your mind. When the inventions (mental handicaps) have been removed, the good will appear automatically. You can then stop demonstrating for there will be nothing to demonstrate over. Balanced people (those in tune with the Infinite) have no need of either heaven or hell. If there were no hell there would be no need of Heaven. Heaven is the natural state of man. It is a state of wholeness, completion and perfection within ones self and has no opposite. It is a state of consciousness which, when it has grown up in us, brings to us the best in life.

A well balanced mind which is produced by controlled thinking is anathema to all germs, disease, poverty and limitations of every kind. What is disease? It is perverted health, and anything that lowers the mental level or lowers nerve energy becomes disease producing. "Disease cannot be its own cause · neither can it be its own cure, and certainly not its own prevention." At the root of every disease is toxemia and at the root of every case of toxemia are all the enervating habits which man himself has built into his own mind and body. What is the remedy? There is only one—to let nature provide her own antidotes and exercise her own prerogative of self-healing. **As we remove the handicaps and clear away the mental and physical obstructions to the good that is constantly moving toward us, Nature heals our bodies and supplies our needs automatically.**

"I and the Father are one." Supply and demand are always equal when man's mind and God's mind are perfectly synchronized or in harmony with each other. **Knowing the Truth is keeping the mind positive to God the good.** "If you know and live the Truth you must be free." God's work is also His purpose. It is to equalize Himself in you. Your work is to keep your mind positive to the good which He is already bestowing upon you. Jesus watched the Father. You do not have to beg for your good but only to receive all the things which the Creative Principle so constantly and willingly gives you.

It is self-evident on the other hand that, since God works through our consciousness, He cannot supply our needs until we cease to be positive to them. **If our consciousness of need is greater than our consciousness of God then the need must continue to expand under that consciousness and we must expect more of the undesirable.** Jesus' formula was to "overcome evil with good."

If the need is to be supplied then the individual's attitude must be reversed. He must lift his vision above the appearance to the fact and keep it there until the Truth forms in him a consciousness of itself. In other words, the positive attitude toward the negative state must be transformed into a **positive attitude toward the positive state.** Why is this so? Because the subconscious builds into our experience those things which are like our consciousness. If we send impulses of discord, inharmony, discontent, poverty, unhappiness, fear, worry, etc., "the subconscious builds us in the image of our order." The law is always to us what we are to It, and it can never be anything else. "As much virtue as there is, so much appears."

If we are going to change our frequency or the subjective tendency of our minds then we must keep on the beam. "Instead of trying to get, we must open ourselves to the whole universe to receive." We must replace struggle with acquiescence. We must replace competition with cooperation. We must let God grow up in us instead of trying to fashion a God of our own. We were made in His Image and to allow that Image to come forth is the "sine qua non" of all spiritual demonstration. When the great adjustment has been made — that is, when the mental attitude has been reversed, we shall discover that the pressure of our need was naught but our supply moving toward us, seeking a positive and receptive state of mind by which to make its Presence known.

The rule is "to acknowledge Me (the positive) in all thy ways, and I will direct thy paths." What does it mean to acknowledge God in all our ways? It means to do something about the ideas and knowledge which we already have. Our peril is that we do so little about what we know. We would rather debate, listen to, or talk about Spiritual ideas than to act upon them. We keep our ideas in the realm of theory. "We are content to deal with them as a juggler plays with ivory balls — he keeps them suspended in the air."

There has been too much random about our way of life, our way of thinking and our way of living. We have failed to commit ourselves to something bigger than ourselves. We have been content to play with ideas rather than to use them. We would rather discuss them than give ourselves to them. It is so much easier to think about our needs (negatives) than to keep our minds open to the Truth or positives. We live with no plan, no purpose and no method. Should we wonder then that metaphysical science has become such a dead-end street for so many, that prayer seems so futile, and that most of our practice has produced nothing but frustration and disappointment? "The lesson which these observations convey, is Be, and not seem."

What is needed to change all this frustration and disappointment is a re-dedication and re-consecration of ourselves to the cause of Life — to make our relation to God totalitarian. We need to make God bigger than ourselves and bigger than anything in our world. We need to ascribe to Him the same importance and power which we formerly ascribed to things. Simply holding an idea will not get us anywhere. We must live it and **Be it.** If we do not live it a distortion will be created. God is peace and if we refuse to live a calm, peaceful, composed and poised life, He cannot make His Presence known to us.

What God is, we must Be. God is to us what we are to ourselves. When we stop the cause of disease, disease goes away. When we stop the cause of poverty, poverty goes away. God cures, when we "take our bloated nothingness out of the path of the Divine Circuits." People are sick from wrong thinking, mal-adjustments in the emotional life and wrong living. Operations remove the effects of our wrong thinking but do not remove the cause. The cause is deep down in the soul. We remove the cause by changing our response, or by reversing our mental attitude from the negative to the positive.

"Choose this day whom ye will serve." Just as our needs were produced by negative mental states (living on our own, which means forgetting God) so they may all be supplied by re-membering, re-turning and re-joining ourselves to the Creative Principle. The great awakening was stated in the words of the Prodigal Son, "I will arise and go unto my Father." The great trinity in Spiritual demonstration is "asking," "believing" and "receiving." In higher metaphysics we would say — Recognition, Realization and Revelation. The inward movement is always from the human mind to the "Christ Mind" and to the super-mind, and the outward movement is from God to Christ, to man. Christ is the distributor of all Heavenly Gifts.

The logical steps in the mastery of any science therefore, is first to discover the Principle — what it is. The second step is to discover how it works — the "modus operandi;" and the third step is to use it the way it works — to cooperate with it. In spiritual work we would say: Find out **what God is;** find out **which way He is going;** and then for successful achievement **go that way.** When we follow these three steps the results will take care of themselves.

WHAT IS GOD?

God is the "Creative Principle" — **the Great Mind** and is symbolized in the Scriptures as The Father. He is the embodiment of all Law, Substance, Intelligence and Power and not only contains all things within Himself but knows nothing outside of Himself by which to divide Himself.

WHAT IS CHRIST?

Christ is the connecting link between man and God and is referred to in the Scriptures as **The Son.** The Christ Mind is mental (aware) in two directions. He is conscious of both God and man.

WHAT IS MAN?

Man is personality and is symbolized in the Scriptures as the carnal, fleshly or human mind. Man is the highest creation of God, not only because he was made in God's Image and Likeness but because he can utilize all three phases of mind to work out his own salvation and to bring into his life everything he desires, or he can by his ignorance and unawareness of the other two phases of mind, deprive himself of the good things of life. If man lives solely by the human mind and its thinking he is then subject to all the deprivations, limitations and ills that flesh and human experience is heir to. To live in heaven, where all his needs are supplied automatically, man must bring these three phases of mind into complete unity and complete cooperation one with the other. This is accomplished by controlled thinking where one recognizes nothing but the Presence and Power of God. When man finally relinquishes the human mind for the Christ Mind, then all things become possible to him.

RECAPITULATION

1. **The source of all supply is God.**

   "Every good and every perfect gift cometh down from above (from above the human mind and its thinking), from the Father of Lights in whom there is no variableness, neither shadow made by turning."

2. **The source of all activity is Christ.**

   "And my God shall supply all your needs according to His riches in glory by CHRIST JESUS."

3. **Man's part is to unite himself with and direct the Creative Energy.**

   When this is done; that is, when man has established a reciprocal action between his mind and the. Mind. of God and provided the states of mind which correspond to his desires, then God will instantly supply his needs.

"If thine eye be single, thy whole body shall be full of light."

"The double-minded man (on the other hand) is unstable in all his ways. Let not that man think that he shall receive anything from the Lord."

Part Two

THIS WORKS

The Father worketh hitherto and I work."
A great man is always willing to be little.
— Emerson.

The object of this book is two-fold: first, to show you how God works; and second, to show you how man can cooperate with God so as to bring about the quickest possible and most desirable and satisfactory results.

God is right now doing every thing for us that needs to be done. "He that keepeth Israel shall neither slumber nor sleep." God is at work all the time seeking to equalize Himself in man. For every human need and demand there is instant, unfailing and self-operative supply. That is God's work.

Man's work is to cooperate with God. "What the son seeth the Father do, that doeth the son also likewise." According to Jesus, man's work is three-fold: To ask — to believe — to receive. Jesus, acting for man, did not try to think, will or declare God into action but He watched what God was doing and did likewise. He watched the Father and was obedient to His Will.

Man's work, therefore, is first, to unite himself with God; second, to move with the activity of God; and third, to provide those states of mind which correspond exactly with his desires. "To the degree that you feel the Creative Mind can and will reproduce your desires, just to that same degree will it manifest Itself in creating them." "We are begirt with laws which execute themselves."

God works through our Requests.

God works through our Beliefs.

God works through Substitution.

God works Now.

God works through Thanksgiving.

GOD WORKS THROUGH OUR REQUESTS.

"'Ask whatsoever ye will – believing – and it shall be done unto you."

Wrapped up in this tremendous statement is both a promise and a formula. In the past we have unconsciously asked for unwanted things and have bound ourselves to them by allowing negative thoughts and images to form and dominate our minds.

We did not know that every thought and emotion was an unconscious demand upon the Universal Substance and that, for the most part, the negative things in our experience were due almost entirely to our unconscious asking. By our failure to collaborate intelligently with God (to direct our minds), we have brought much sickness and financial distress into our lives. · In the past we have allowed persons, places and things to determine our states of consciousness and to control our lives. We shall henceforth change those negative conditions by changing our perspective. Like George Müller, in the story at the beginning of our book, we must **utterly die** to the world or human consciousness. St. Paul said, "Reckon ye yourselves to be dead unto sin (the negative) and alive unto God" — the good. Instead of being the victims of negative states of mind, we shall henceforth create positive states and live in them.

The promise is that "ye shall ask what ye will and it shall be done unto you. . . . If thou canst believe, all things are possible to him that believeth." "Intelligent asking and intelligent believing," says Lucius Humphrey, "unite the human mind, the Christ Mind and the God Mind in you, thereby creating whatsoever ye will." And Sir James Jeans said, "An idea in the mind produces things outside the mind, and things outside the mind produce ideas in the mind." In other words, **whatsoever we ask for must first be formed in the mind before it can be formed outside the mind.** According to Jesus, we must pray from the standpoint of having what we ask for. We must pray for what we believe we have, instead of praying for what we believe we do not have. "The soul answers never by words, but by the thing itself that is inquired after."

The fact that we supplicate God is proof that we are conscious of some lack in our lives. The lack represents. a negative condition which can be supplied or overcome only by a corresponding positive condition. Our asking therefore should be in the form of an opposite image held steadfastly in the mind, thus turning the energy, which erstwhile had been feeding and holding us in bondage to a negative state of mind, into new, positive and constructive channels. The new image, if maintained and held steadfastly without opposition or interruption, will in time counteract all that the negative condition created and produce a new effect.

"Let this mind be in you which was also in Christ Jesus, who, being in the form of God, thought it not robbery to be equal with God." "Let every soul be subject unto Higher powers. For there is no power but of God."

Since the human mind, unaided by a higher power, is insufficient to create or demonstrate anything for itself it must have recourse to the Higher Intelligence of the Christ Mind, which, with God is able to do all things. Now if you will turn again to page 29 you will see how the positive image overcomes the negative image. The asking is done, or the image is projected by the human mind. It is then received and held by the Christ Mind in the soul (through our faith and belief) and from there automatically attracts from God the elements like the elements in itself and is given back to man in form. "Revelation is the disclosure of the soul." "The purpose of our asking therefore is to unite the human mind with the Christ Mind, thus making us conscious creators of all the things we desire and wish."

"Ye shall know the Truth," said Jesus, "and the Truth shall make you free." That is just like saying that white is white, black is black and two times two are four. The true metaphysician does not reason, argue, petition nor beg God for what he already has. He acknowledges that he has it, thanks God for it and takes it. To him, God is God. White is white. Water is wet and two times two are four. Knowing that spiritual things are spiritually discerned and working from the basis of the child or Christ state of Mind, he does not think of all the false combinations in which ignorant and unenlightened minds declare that two and two might be something else. To him, **God is.** Two times two are always four and can never be anything else.

Is the body sick? Is the pocket book empty? If you admit these conditions aren't you saying that two and two make five or something else? If you proclaim the lie, does that change the fact? If you proclaim the Truth does that change the condition? Does anything happen when you declare the Truth? Does your declaration change anything? Can it change anything but yourself? Can it do anything other than to bring your own mind into alignment with fact?

What is the Truth? The Truth is the positive quality of every negative condition. Did two and two make four before you said it or after you said it? Does your declaration of the fact make it so or was it so before you proclaimed it? Why did Jesus say "Thank you Father," before there was any tangible

23

evidence of the answer? Was He trying to create something or was He proving something that was already a fact in his own consciousness? How does one "know the Truth?" **By choosing the positive quality represented by a negative quality and staying the mind upon it until it forms in him a consciousness of itself.** How does the Truth make us free? **By moving with the power and directing it into positive channels.**

"I, God, change not." White is always white. The Christ is the same yesterday, today and forever. The ignorant man says two and two make five. I am sick, I am poor, I am unhappy. Does the five change the four? Can the lie prevail when he knows that two and two do make four? "Awake, thou that sleepest and Christ shall give thee Light." Knowing the truth is bringing the conscious and subconscious minds into perfect alignment with the fact. The fact becomes form (the Truth makes us free) when man becomes the fact in action. "This energy does not descend into individual life on any other condition than entire possession. It comes to the lowly and simple: it comes to whosoever will put off what is foreign and proud."

GOD WORKS THROUGH OUR BELIEFS.

The law of the Lord is perfect."

Divine Law is the servant of man. It was given to man not only to create those things which he desires and wishes but to enable him to overcome all the negative and undesirable conditions in his life. Because God's Law is fixed, rigid and mathematical it can always be depended upon. If it is used positively it will bring only good into man's life. If it is used negatively it will bring evil. **The Law is to us what we are to it.** It will always respond to us according to our believing thought. Whatever we believe in without doubt the law is that thing, and will produce it in our experience according to the fixity of our vision and the intensity of our thought.

"As you believe so shall you receive." The Law being Impersonal does not know good nor 'evil. It is so designed that it must make you and your circumstances in the image of your beliefs. If you believe that a draught of fresh air has the power to give you a cold then any draught of air is a law unto that thing. If you believe that golden rod has the power to give you hay fever then for you golden rod is a law unto hay fever. You will be subject to hay fever every time golden rod appears because you are subject to whatever you believe in.

"Whatsoever a man soweth, that shall he also reap." If you believe in sickness and health then you are not only subject to both but you will manifest both. If you believe in success and failure you will be subject to both. There will be times when you will succeed and other times when you will fail. If you believe in wealth and poverty then you will be subject to both. Sometimes you will have one and sometimes you will have the other. If you believe that some men are honest and others are dishonest then you will attract both into your life. Some will take from you and others will give to you. If you fear thieves you will attract them to your world. They must come to you by the law of your belief. Job said, "the thing I feared came upon me." He believed it would come upon him and it did. Fear is faith in evil. It is a negative belief. What we believe in, we demonstrate on all occasions. **By the law of belief we have attracted to ourselves all that we have and by the same law we have separated ourselves from those things which we do not have.**

25

The world is made up of two classes of people: those who have everything they need because they are positive to them, and those who, because they entertain negative states of mind, deprive themselves of the good things of life. In the first case we have healthy, happy, prosperous and successful people. In the second case we have miserable, diseased and unsuccessful people. Positive people meet the problems of life squarely and courageously. Negative people meet them with fear and doubt. The law is infallible and we should not be disappointed if it works the way we expect it to. "The law has no choice but to obey its own terms."

"God's work is finished. He is the Law. He is the supply. Our work is to obey the law, to receive and distribute the supply." If we have been going in the wrong direction for a long time we must now turn around and go in the right direction. It may take a little while for us to get turned around **but turn we must.** When Jesus said, "Turn the other cheek," "Give your cloak with your coat" and "Go the second mile" He meant that we were to go all the way with the Law.

How do we do that? **By taking absolute control of the mind and by replacing every negative state with a positive state.** It would also involve the formulation of new habits of thinking by watching our thoughts and by refusing to give power to adverse and negative conditions, and by refusing to allow ourselves to be the victims of our circumstances. As we cease to give power to the negatives by refusing to think about or entertain them, we are calling forth the higher use of the law for the fulfillment of our desires. As our minds become more and more positive to the Truth our material and other conditions will become more and more satisfactory. To obey the law and use it positively and constructively continues to be the rule for all successful achievement.

GOD WORKS THROUGH SUBSTITUTIONS

"Be not overcome of evil, but overcome evil with good."

The best way to get rid of the evil in our lives is by refusing to entertain it. The best way to destroy the consciousness of poverty is to **cultivate the consciousness of wealth.** The best way to destroy the consciousness of sickness is to **cultivate the consciousness of health.** The wise gardener works to make his crop so abundant that it will overshadow · the weeds. If we spent all our time in trying to get rid of the negatives in our lives, and nothing more, we would finally succeed in producing a state of consciousness, devoid of goodness as well as evil and it would be good for nothing.

St. Paul said, "Overcome evil with good." We must substitute. We must choose the Truth and stick to it. When the positive idea is introduced, the negative idea dies away. "Except ye be converted . . . ye shall in no wise enter the Kingdom of Heaven." What is conversion? It is merely a change of allegiance from the negative side of life to the positive side. It is both a change of mind and a change of self. It is not acquiring new things but a shift in mind so that you can use the things which you already have. When you are converted you simply align yourself with the positive elements in life and make them supreme. Man must take the initiative. He must not only put himself and his mind on the positive side but he must make it the winning side, the dominant side.

"I find then a law, that when I would do good, evil is present with me." Since we have proved to ourselves that we cannot work successfully in the human mind, we must let it die by refusing to use it to think with. Jesus said, "Call no man on earth your Father." What did He mean? He meant that we must adopt a new Father (Higher State of Mind) "and inherit goodness instead of evil." Jesus' method was to cultivate the good instead of restricting evil. "Do, instead of do not." "He set people to doing right instead of escaping wrong." The human consciousness will die as we cultivate the Christ Consciousness.

Your business and my business in Spiritual work is to mentally get back of all the deformities and imperfections which appear, and by our positive attitude toward the Truth, transmute them all into terms of perfection. We do this in the same way that the moving picture operator changes the picture on the screen. He does not deal directly with the picture itself or the light but changes the film. When the film is changed the picture changes automatically.

Man's screen is his world and his life. It is his body, his home, his friends, his associates, his business and his environment. His projector is his consciousness which of course is always responsible for his outer circumstances. By his consciousness he has attracted to himself all that he has or is.

Now let us suppose that the pictures on man's screen are not to his liking. What must he do? Can he change the pictures by working with conditions — stewing, fretting, worrying and fearing? No, because that would only create more ugliness and imperfection in his world. There is only one thing he can do and that is to go within his projector (consciousness) and change the film or image of his thought. If he has been experiencing negative conditions in his environment, then he must replace them with the positive images which the negatives represent. He must select the picture which he wants — first in the form of a mental image and then he must hold it and use it until it expresses itself in material conditions.

The thing that most people do not seem to understand is that the picture is never on the screen but always in the mind or projector. It can only be changed by inserting a different film. There is only one Light which shines through every projector but the Light is never responsible for the pictures we show. The Light is always pure whether the picture we project be good or bad. **"This is the true light which lighteth every man that cometh into the world."** The Light is never to blame. Being impersonal it will project a good picture or a bad one. What appears on the screen only changes its appearance. The film, by and of itself, does not and cannot change the Light. The Light is God and will project any picture which man holds before it. Thus when man substitutes positive films (states of mind) for negative ones, he will get different pictures and different appearances. What the world commonly calls a healing will take place.

Jesus said, "Let your Light so shine that men may see your **good works.**" And again, "I am the Light of the World." Right in the midst of your most trying hour, your deepest sorrow, your most grievous illness, your greatest anxiety and your most terrifying fear, God's Light is shining, searching out all the dark places in your life. He is in the midst of your greatest failure offering you success. He is in the midst of your most vexing problem offering you a solution. He is in the midst of your depleted bank account offering you supply.

That is paradoxical you say, for how can a God who is love and who perceives only good in His creation allow such limitations, deformities and defects to appear? He allows them only in the sense that He has given you free choice and volition to think and act as you please. He has given you the power to see what you wish to see and to believe what you wish to believe. If, therefore, you put His pure light through negative, human films, you will bring out imperfect pictures or results. If you pervert His Light and Power you will get perverse and distorted conditions.

Is it God's fault when you get imperfect pictures? Do your pictures change God or His Creation? Not at all. "I, God, change not." How then are human needs to be met? **By transforming our negative states of mind into positive ones.** It makes no difference what we may think to the contrary, there is one thing certain and patent to all those who have eyes to see and that is — that **a negative state of mind simply cannot produce positive and successful ideas.** It is wise, therefore, if one wants desirable results to transform every negative state into a positive one.

How is that to be done? **By being so conscious of God's Presence and so positive to the good that we are un-conscious of anything in our lives that is unlike God.** Instead of human limitations and imperfections we see the divine possibilities in everything and everybody. Instead of sickness we see God's wholeness and rely absolutely upon His Power to bring it forth. Instead of criticism we see God's Love and Divine Completion. In His Consciousness the other fellow becomes our other self. Instead of ignorance, we see Divine Wisdom, Knowledge and Power. Instead of scarcity and poverty we see God's Infinite and Eternal Wealth. Instead of frustration, futility and failure, we contemplate God's boundless and unlimited Resources. Instead of fear we practice confidence. Instead of weakness, vacillation and indecision we contemplate God's steadfastness, security and strength. "Neither circumcision, nor uncircumcision availeth anything, but a new creature." The new creature is none other than our ability to look beyond appearances until we can see ourselves as we are.

GOD WORKS IN THE NOW

"Say not ye, there are yet four months and then cometh the harvest? behold, I say unto you, Lift up your eyes, and look on the fields, for they are white already to harvest."

The chief difference between rational theology and false theology is essentially a difference in tense. One is claiming your good now and the other is preparing for it in the future. The first is accepting what you already have while the second is trying to demonstrate it. It is the difference between unloading the ship that is already moored at the dock and waiting for an imaginary ship to come in. It is the difference between seeking things and having things seek you. It is the difference between seeing things as they are and seeing them as they appear.

"Now is the accepted time." "It is what we do in the present that counts; the past is gone, and the future is not ready to be acted upon. Give your. time, your talent and your power to that which is now at hand and you will do things worth while; you will not waste time upon what you expect to do; but you will turn all your energies upon that which you now can do; results will positively follow. Instead of giving anxious thought to the bridge we may have to cross we should give scientific thought to the increase of present ability and power; thus we make ourselves fully competent to master every occasion that may be met."

When you are told not to talk about the four months which the human mind says are necessary to produce a harvest, you are warned not to put a time limit upon what God can do for you. It means literally that you are not to consider the processes of sowing and growing but to expect everything NOW. The grain you are requited to gather is already ripe. It is ripe. Do you hear? The fields are white. They are already to pluck.

"Behold! Look again." Are you a grower or a harvester? Do you "have eyes and see not?" "Say not ye, there are yet four months and then cometh the harvest." Rather consider the difference between now and then, between reaping and growing, between Revelation and demonstration, between Being and becoming. What does it mean when you are told to "lift up your eyes and look?" Can you see the Higher Good planned for you? Can you accept it? How do you pray? Do you petition or beg God to do something for you or do you thank Him because you already have it? Yes—it is the tense in Spiritual work which makes all the difference in the results. Either the field is planted or you must plant it. Either the grain is ripe or you must ripen it. Which will you have? There is an old slogan which says, "Eventually—why not now." It is NOW or never. "Now are we the sons of God." "Now is the accepted time." "Now is the day of salvation." "The Kingdom of Heaven is at hand." It is now. Everything is NOW. Your ship is in and you can unload it whenever you choose. The law of Jesus Christ is not a law of demonstration but of fulfillment. "I am come that ye might have life and have it more abundantly." I am here. "I am come that your joy might be full." **"Full"**—do you hear? "All that the Father hath is mine,"—is yours. It is yours NOW and only awaits a corresponding state of consciousness to bring it into being. "But man postpones or remembers; he does not live in the present, but with reverted eye laments the past, or, heedless of the riches that surround him, stands on tip toe to foresee the future. He cannot be happy and strong · until he too lives with nature in the present, above time."

"I am the Resurrection and the Life." You do not have to die to be immortal. You are immortal now. You are living a life that has no end. Right now your life is filled to the brim with luxury, health, wealth, power, happiness, peace, substance, prosperity and contentment. If you are not enjoying your share of these good things it is because through your negative images and thinking you are causing God to bring to you something else. The baptism of the Holy Spirit is what happens to you when you stop being that which you thought you were and begin to be that which YOU ARE. To lose the outward manifestation insures the inward revelation, yea, the fulfillment of the promise. "He dwelleth with you, and shall be in you." "He taketh away the first that He may establish the second."

The Kingdom of God cometh not with observation. Why not? Because it is with you NOW. It is IN YOU. It is YOU. "In Him we live, move and have our being." "The Kingdom of Heaven IS AT HAND." It is HERE NOW. "IT IS WITH MEN." That which is already HERE does not have to come. There is no place for it to come from. You cannot go to WHERE YOU ARE. You can only discover where you are. That WHICH IS, does not have to be demonstrated but PROVED. It does not have to be transmitted but revealed. It does not have to be reflected but individualized—Personified. That WHICH IS must be RECOGNIZED, LIVED IN and USED. It cannot lie brought here as a result of our thinking, praying or demonstrating. We can only wake up to it. We can only become aware that it is.

"For now we see through a glass, darkly; but then, face to face; now I know in part; but then I shall know even as also I am known."

"Let this mind be in you which was also in Christ Jesus." The human mind, unaided by the Christ Mind, does not see things as they are but only as they appear, and appearances as we know are deceiving. "Spiritual things are spiritually discerned." They must be seen through the Spiritual senses with the Mind of Christ. When Jesus said, "My Kingdom is not of this world," He meant that we could not express His Life, Health, Substance and Power without His Mind. Since God is Spirit and His Kingdom is a Spiritual Kingdom both must be contacted on spiritual terms.

"Awake thou that sleepest, and arise from the dead (darkness) and Christ shall give thee light." Since the darkness of human understanding is the only problem there is, it can be overcome only as we let in the Light. As the Light grows we shall see things as they are. We shall see them face to face. We shall know as we are known. "Ye are the light of the world" (your world). A city that is set upon a hill cannot be hid. "Ye have eyes," said Jesus, "and see not, ears have ye and hear not." To try to discern Spiritual things without His Mind (Light) is like going into a dark room to find an object. Without the light one sees but faintly the dim outlines of the objects in the room but cannot discern clearly anything that is there. It is almost impossible to find what he is looking for. The objects are all there but he does not see them as they are. Without the Light he has a limited vision of everything in the room.

"Then shall the eyes of the blind be opened, and the ears of the deaf unstopped." The vision of the single eye is true. In the midst of the most imperfect, malformed and pain-racked body is perfection. Within the meanest, most murderous man alive is God. Under the most crippled enterprise is God. Over the most helpless situation is God. He is both the visible imperfections and the invisible perfection. There could be no imperfection without perfection. The imperfections are but our failure to see clearly the Eternal Perfection which never changes. Like the objects in the dark room without the light, Reality does not come into full view.

"Beholding Perfection, it is decreed for me." "Wherever you can vision perfection," says Celia C. Cole, "you can attain it. As far and high as you are able to see, so far and high can you go. Your ability is always equal to your vision. The trick, of course, is to be able to brush aside appearances, to go right through them to the spiritual fact back of them, like pushing away the more or less imperfect instrument that is a lamp and beholding the wonder of light. Then to realize what the Spiritual fact is, as a scientist knows what his formula is, and to stand upon it, immovable, undisturbed, no matter what appears. By using the power we have to see good, more will come. By observing the working of the law in every happening, you develop spiritual perception. Use it in the little things of every day—then it will come automatically for the big ones."

"What will you have," said Emerson, "pay for it and take it." When you go to Honolulu you do not have to demonstrate the climate, plants, swimming and volcanoes. You only have to see what is already there and enjoy it. When you are in Hawaii you are under the laws of Hawaii and no longer under the Jaws of your home state. Then what would you think if you saw a man in Honolulu walking around its streets declaring that he was in Honolulu and affirming the sunshine, orchids, gardenias, etc., etc.? Wouldn't you think that there was something wrong with such a man? Wouldn't you think it strange that he did not use and enjoy what he already had instead of talking about it?

Then what about the Truth student who spends his days and nights declaring the Truth and affirming that he is in the Kingdom of God and does nothing about it? Is he any different from the man in Honolulu? Is it not true that "a house divided against itself shall fall?" How can one enjoy Honolulu unless he does it unthoughtfully, unless he acts as though he were there? And how can you enjoy the Kingdom of God unless you proceed along the same lines? You do not need to take a train nor a boat to the Kingdom of God. You do not even need to get anyone to put you in it. You are already there. You must stay in it unthoughtfully in the same way that you stay where you are right now.

When you jump into a pool of water it is the business of the water to make you wet. The water substantiates itself. When you go to the North Pole it is the business of the climate there to make you cold. It substantiates itself. When you go to the tropics it is the business of the tropical climate to make you warm. When you go into the Kingdom of God (keep your mind focused on the good—the positive) it is the business of the Kingdom of God to supply you with everything you desire and need. Jesus said, "all these things shall be added unto you." If you go into the Kingdom of God it will not only set you free but keep you free as long as you remain in it.

In the Kingdom of God you would not declare that there was no sickness nor poverty nor anything negative, because in the Kingdom of God there would be nothing for negatives to act with. The perfection and good things of the Kingdom of God have already been demonstrated for you. It is the Father's good pleasure to give you the things of the Kingdom of God and to keep giving them to you as long as you remain in it (are positive to the good), just as it is the business of water to keep you wet as long as you stay in the water. If you go back to your home state however you lose sight of the things in Honolulu, just as when you go back to your human mind you lose sight of the things in the Kingdom of God. Jesus said, "Remain within my love." "Continue in my word," — "Abide in me." The secret of continuous supply is not to allow the mind to be divided against itself. He will keep him in a perfect state of health, wealth, peace, power and abundance whose mind is stayed upon God — the good — the positive.

GOD WORKS THROUGH THANKSGIVING

"With thanksgiving let your requests be made known unto God." — "In everything give thanks."

It is our purpose in this book to give you an infallible and dependable method of practice which will not only produce new ideas and increase your power, but tile means by which all personal problems can be solved, and by which all personal desires and wishes can be fulfilled. It is such a simple formula that a child can use it with splendid results. Indeed we do not know of another method which has such tremendous power and such unlimited possibilities. It is the law of asking, believing and receiving all in one word — THANKSGIVING. "Faith is the substance of things hoped for" and Thanksgiving is "the evidence of things not seen." Faith and Thanksgiving go hand in hand, they are in fact the handmaidens of the Lord.

We have talked much in this book about the necessity of bringing the three phases of mind into complete cooperation one with the other and we are frank to say that there is no other method so successful in accomplishing this as the simple practice of THANKSGIVING. If rightly practiced there is no other means which so effectively harmonizes the human, Christ and Super minds for the purpose of fulfilling one's desires.

"Enter into His gates with THANKSGIVING and into His courts with PRAISE; and be thankful unto Him." Few students realize that the key to successful practice and living is to be found in gratitude and praise, and conversely, that the greatest thieves to happiness and abundance are ingratitude and complaining. After all the metaphysical theories have been written, and all the philosophical platitudes have been spoken, the thing that really does the work and sets the law in operation is THANKSGIVING. When everything else fails, Thanksgiving will succeed. It will succeed because it is mathematically correct, and because it is the method which Jesus used.

THINGS TO BE REMEMBERED ABOUT THANKSGIVING

1.   The ultimate goal of all spiritual practice is to be so fully conscious of God's Presence that we are unconscious of anything unlike God.

2.   Since God is the Source of all supply and the giver of every good and perfect gift, then the closer we live to God the more good things and the more spiritual benefits we shall receive from Him.

3.   The best method for living close to God is the practice of whole-souled gratitude. The mind that is always grateful is never in need.

4.   If we are grateful for the good things we have now we shall receive more in the future. If we are grateful for everything we shall constantly receive more of everything.

5.   The perpetual attitude and feeling of THANKS-GIVING brings the mind of man and the Mind of God into perfect reciprocal action. Gratitude keeps man's mind open toward God.

6.   The grateful mind is a power-full mind. It is not only more efficient in everything, but always accomplishes everything it sets out to do. It is fatigueless, buoyant, joyous, alive.

7.   The thankful mind is always positive to the good. It looks for the best and brings the best out of everything. Seeing only the good, it causes "everything to produce good."

8.   The grateful soul is accumulative. The practice of Thanksgiving keeps the mind in the ascending tendency and the higher the mind goes the greater will be its possessions. The more grateful it is the more power it will have.

9.   The thankful soul lives in the NOW and expects everything in the present. It does not worry about nor live in the future.

10.   "In love is love reflected." The grateful person expects the best from everything and receives the best. He attracts better friends, better deals and better opportunities.

11.   The grateful soul is always a satisfied soul. Drawing its substance and life from within, it is always well.

12.   The thankful soul is a productive soul. Living close to the source of all, it not only attracts more, but produces more in every sphere of activity.

13.   The grateful soul is a regenerative soul. In the consciousness of real gratitude, healing force is always at work counter-acting negative conditions.

14.   The grateful soul is a balanced soul. In whole-souled gratitude, supply and demand are always equal. "The moment resistance (ingratitude) gives way, there is a great inrush of whatever is needed."

If there is such a thing as a short cut to Heaven it is to be found in the Prayer of Thanksgiving. Genuine gratitude not only opens the entire being to God but frees the mind from those undesirable and seemingly stronger, negative thoughts which have made it impossible for us to accept the things for which we have prayed. We know now that all negative states must be transposed into positive states before our prayers can be answered. When Jesus said, "Pray without ceasing," He was not telling us to beg, supplicate or beseech God to do certain things for us but to cultivate a deep sense of whole-souled gratitude within ourselves. To be perpetually thankful for everything is fulfilling the command to "pray without ceasing."

We declare then, that the prayer of faith, or acting upon what we ALREADY HAVE is at once the most effective, successful and productive of all methods of prayer. It is really praying in three ways at the same time, or more literally speaking, it is three prayers in one. It is the prayer of Asking, Believing and Receiving. It is Recognition, Realization and Revelation.

Jesus understood this method of prayer when, before there was any tangible evidence of the answer He said, **"I thank Thee, Father, that thou hast heard me and I know that thou hearest me always."** It was not His words alone that caused the Power to come into manifestation but His belief that what He had thanked the Father for was already there. "I thank thee, Father" is the full recognition and realization that the thing is taking place right HERE and NOW. It doesn't make any difference what system you use, how much you know or how much you pray, the object of your prayer cannot become yours until you have thanked God for it. "You will not reap the full benefits of the law until you begin to throw all your forces on the positive, constructive side."

"To perceive an idea, to grasp it, to hold and use it, continues to be the rule for successful accomplishment." There are many definitions of prayer but the greatest and most comprehensive one is, that **it is the practice of the Presence of God** which of course is the PRAYER OF THANKSGIVING. First, we mentally lay hold of the good we desire. We recognize that it is NOW. Then, second we practice absolute confidence in God's desire and ability to bestow it and in Christ's activity to bring it forth by thanking Him for it. It is our gratitude that makes it so.

"The prayer of faith," said St. James, "shall save the sick." "Be of good cheer, thy faith hath made thee whole." What is faith? It is a settled state of feeling. It is ABSOLUTE CONFIDENCE in God, our word and the Law. **When our faith in God is absolute, our prayers work for us because we are channels for divine action.** Instead of seeking things as aforetime, things will now be seeking us. Having become magnets for good by establishing positive states of mind within ourselves there is no longer anything that can keep our good from finding us. We now attract it by virtue of what we are. Having entered into a state of balance or unity with God, we attract from the outer world everything needful for a perfect and harmonious existence. "He that hath the Spirit (positive state of mind) hath the sign also." God's riches flow to us from EVERY source and whole-souled gratitude opens wide the mind to receive.

Is there a momentous and important decision which you must make? Do you need guidance and wisdom? Then say to the need each time it comes to your mind: "Father, I thank Thee," and see how quickly the guidance will come.

Is there a problem in your home, office, business or personal life which you have been unable to solve? Then say to it each time you think of it, "Father, I thank Thee," and see how quickly the solution will come.

Are you depressed, anxious or fearful over some situation which you do not seem able to control? Then repeat these words "God, I thank Thee," and see how quickly your feelings will change. "In everything, give thanks."

Are you so sick that nothing seems to do you any good? Then say every time your sickness comes to mind "Father I thank Thee," and see how soon you will feel better and how quickly you will begin to improve.

Are you in debt and need money? Then say, "Father, I thank Thee" each time the need comes into your mind and watch the money come.

Give thanks instead of complaining. Give thanks instead of fearing. Give thanks instead of worrying. Give thanks instead of wondering. "God is a very present help in time of trouble," but He cannot help you unless you accept His help on Spiritual terms. You must approach Him from the standpoint of having what you ask for. You must accept His help through positive states of mind and through your attitude of Praise and Thanksgiving. **If there is nothing in your consciousness that doubts your word, or that is unlike God, then He will supply everything in abundant measure.** "There is no great and no small to the soul that maketh all." Seven dollars or seven million dollars, headache or cancer — it is all the same to God.

The promise is that "whatsoever ye shall ask the Father IN MY NAME (nature), He will give it to you." You do not have to beg God for anything, you only have to enter His nature (positive state of mind) and you can take from the universe anything you wish.

When you are in the nature of Christ you will not even have to ask for it. It will be added unto you. "Before ye call I will answer and while ye are yet speaking I will hear." "And they shall see His face; and His name (nature) shall be on their foreheads (in their minds); His nature shall be their nature." Is there anything unusual about a potter producing pottery, about a jeweler producing jewelry, about a baker producing bread, a composer producing music? Is there anything unusual about a man with the Mind of Christ doing the works of Jesus?

To be in His nature is to be in Heaven and to have all things added unto you. To be out of His nature is to be in the world and to have to fight and struggle for your good.

A fig tree without figs has no reason for being.

It were better for you not to know these things than to know them and fail to apply them.

"Be ye doers of the word and not hearers only deceiving your own selves."

"There hath not failed one word of all His good promises."

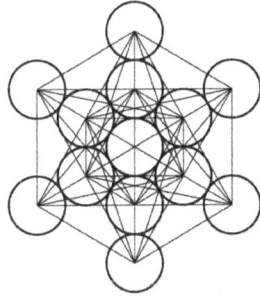

Raisa - Mystic Alchemist

Energy Healing, Chakra Alignment, Sacred Geometry, Sound Healing

Tammy:
I was blessed with a healing session by Raisa last week. She felt like a friend and like-minded gentle soul with comforting Mother Mary essence pouring through her words. Raisa was so in-tuned to my blocks and traumas held within my field. She used her connection to ascended masters I've resonated with such as Yeshua, Mother Mary, Mary Magdalene, Lady Vesta & Amethyst and archangels Metatron, Michael and others to help clear these.

I was able to address childhood trauma situations to flip the stuck energy I've held onto over the years. She also picked up on a few traumatic past-life scenes that have affected my current life. I am an intuitive energy healer who truly felt the shift and healing within. I now feel so much lighter and have clarity regarding my path.

So much love and gratitude to you both, Raisa and Barry for presenting her to my world! (More Testimonials on following Pages)

Contact Raisa to book an Energy Healing
or Chakra Alignment session:
www.RaisinYourIsness.com
raisinyourisness@hotmail.com

Shannon:
This BEAUTIFUL sister...our Raisa... is a treasure beyond compare! After my experience in my personal session with Raisa... the ABSOLUTE confirmation I received, that could ONLY be confirmed by HER mind you... this session solidified EVERYTHING for me. I KNOW that this sister... she is a formidable, magnificent & IRREPLACEABLE component in this Earth plane story we all are invested in! IF YOU ARE DRAWN TO HER FOLLOW YOUR HEART

No other can do what SHE is gifted to do for YOU... YES YOU!

I LOVE YOU dear sister! I am forever grateful for what only you could do and DID for me! I would have happily paid any price for what you gave me! I URGE YOU ALL to schedule a session with this beloved one!

P.S. thank you Barry for sharing her with us all!

∞

Natasha:
I would like to thank Barry for introducing us to Raisa. I have had 2 consultations with her in the last month and I am in total awe of what transpired. Raisa is such a beautiful caring soul! She connected with me as though she has known me forever. Her love and dedication in assisting others is so touching. I had an amazing experience and some profound healing. I received a message from Jeshua which brought tears to my eyes. I could feel the LOVE in the message that was given to me and I will remember and cherish His message forever. Raisa has really helped me in confronting fears, trauma and past life karma. I have found the reason for my skin problems which I never would have thought it'd be possible. It is amazing what guilt and shame from past lives can actually do to your body. Her healing and that from our Angelic beings has really made a huge difference in my life. I can feel it in my energy. Raisa has a lovely sense of humour, always reminding you not to take life and yourself so seriously. I really feel like a heavy weight has been lifted off my soul. Thank you so much! Much Love!

∞

Ariel:

Raisa... Divine Raisa... You are a Treasure to this Life, and I thank All That Is, and this also Treasured YT channel for the priceless blessing which was our session this AM. Every moment of the session was a fractal explosion of wonderful intuitive & divinely guided perfection. I honor your sincere, caring, graceful, playful, soothing, encouraging, transformational, empowering, and so beautiful demonstration / embodiment of Goddess energy and presence. I am so honored & thankful to have been guided to You. To have invested in the patience, time, energy, and resources to share sacred healing and uplifting time with You. I will remember the session Always. And I will look forward to any and all ways our Creator deems it harmonious to connect again. I could go on and on and on, so please accept my parting acknowledgment of your blessing to this realm, my Heart & Spirt, my Life, and the Lives of all those who may be positively impacted via your assistance. Blessings, and Gratitude, a thousand times over and over again. Namaste... Namaste... Namaste...

∞

B.G.

I have just finished a healing session with Raisa. The experience was remarkable! I am still buzzing! I heard about her from this channel, so thank you deeply Barry!

Raisa is so lovely to talk to, and intuitively guided, knows how to get to the hidden roots of our issues. She calls upon ascended masters, archangels and such to do deep energetic clearing and healing work. It was like being guided through the deep layers of myself, releasing the things that don't serve me and filling every cell with light. I purged, and I absorbed new energy, and came out feeling uplifted and renewed. Raisa helped me to find things in myself that I had been cut off from, and to heal wounds I had tried to bury. She has also given me helpful ideas to continue to improve things my life.

I am so blessed to have found Raisa, and ever grateful for the healing work she has done. She is as authentic as they come. Truly an earth angel! Thank you, thank you, thank you!

▶ YouTube

YouTube Channels of Interest:

Giving Voice to the Wisdom of the Ages

Over 5,000 audios, hundreds of
Spiritual and Metaphysical
audio books including
Robert A Russell, Dr Murdo MacDonald Bayne,
Napoleon Hill, Jeshua, Kryon and many more.

I AM Meditations and Affirmations

Hundreds of I AM Meditations,
Daily affirmations and more.

Raisin' Your Isness

Metaphysical Musings, Channelings,
Sound Healing Songs

www.ingramcontent.com/pod-product-compliance
Lightning Source LLC
Chambersburg PA
CBHW021349090426
42742CB00008B/797